UNLOCK YOUR INHERITANCE

UNLOCK YOUR INHERITANCE

It's Our Money–Why Are We Waiting?

A close look at the causes of delay in deceased estates, with constructive suggestions for avoiding them

Raymond Hebson

W. Foulsham & Co. Ltd.

London • New York • Toronto • Cape Town • Sydney

W. Foulsham & Company Limited
Yeovil Road, Slough, Berkshire, SL1 4JH

ISBN 0-572-01055-9

Copyright © 1987 Raymond Hebson

All rights reserved.
The Copyright Act (1956) prohibits (subject to certain
very limited exceptions) the making of copies of any
copyright work or of a substantial part of such a work,
including the making of copies by photocopying or
similar process. Written permission to make a copy
or copies must therefore normally be obtained from the
publisher in advance. It is advisable also to consult
the publisher if in any doubt as to the legality of any
copying which is to be undertaken.

Printed in Great Britain at
St Edmundsbury Press,
Bury St Edmunds

CONTENTS

Chapter 1 Introduction 7
2 Information 10
3 Anticipation — the key to progress 15
4 The Grant 17
5 Inheritance Tax 20
6 Income Tax and Capital Gains Tax 23
7 Advertising for Claims 26
8 Missing Relatives 28
9 Assets — sell or keep? 30
10 Estate Accounts 32
11 Papers in Disarray 34
12 Professional Executors 36
13 Snags 39
14 Covering Up 40
15 Decisions 43
16 Picking up the threads 45
17 Difficult Relationships 48
18 What of the Future? 50

Appendix A Information Checklist 52
B Estate Administration Checklist 54
C Decision Tree 57
D Estate Control 58

Index 59

Chapter 1

INTRODUCTION

"Why are we waiting?"

This question must have been asked thousands — perhaps millions — of times down the ages, yet delay in winding up deceased estates is still prevalent. Why should this be? Book after excellent book has been written about the duties of executors, about the law of succession and about all the associated aspects and technicalities; but the simple fact remains that estates often seem to drag on far longer than they should before the money is paid out.

Seem to drag on? Yes, because in some cases delay cannot be avoided. In others it can and should. But it can often be very difficult to pinpoint the exact cause of the trouble because executors, being human, are not as a rule over-anxious to come up with facts, such as failure to deal with correspondence, which will brand them as inefficient. And the purpose of this book is not to attribute blame; still less is it to add yet one more volume on executorship law and accounts to the admirable ones already available. The purpose is to seek out the causes of delay, examine them in as much detail as seems necessary and try to find remedies.

Before getting down to the details of the various factors which are liable to affect the administration of an estate, it is worth giving some thought to the background against which the work of administration is normally carried out. And at the outset it should be recognised that dealing with an estate is hardly ever good fun. At best the work, or more likely parts of it, may be quite interesting, but at other times the job can be extremely tedious and perhaps a great strain, destroying any initial optimism and enthusiasm which the executor may have had. This state of affairs is by no means exceptional, and in a case of extreme weariness the specifics suggested in this book may be of no avail. The only satisfactory course when this stage has been reached is to bring in a new broom to help or take over.

Professional executors are, of course, paid for what they do. It is not unreasonable to expect high standards from them. But there are relatively few professional men and women who spend their whole time on executorship work. And at times some of their other work, not connected with executorship, may be very demanding in terms of time limits. An accountant, for instance, must prepare a set of company accounts in time for them to be duly circulated before the company meeting at which they are to be presented. A solicitor must have his conveyance ready for completion by a fixed date or his case ready for hearing on the appointed day. So when a professional man comes under pressure, what happens? The work which must be done to meet the deadlines gets done first, and the deceased estates, not being subject to any time limits, get put off. Sometimes the same estate, if it presents time-consuming problems, gets put off again and again. There is no simple remedy for this. It is a counsel of perfection to suggest that in every professional office which handles estates there should be at least one person who does nothing else but estate work and is therefore unaffected by the time limits. This would mean that, in an office in which there was not enough executorship work to keep such a person fully occupied, idle time would have to be carried, and as a result the fees for administering estates would rocket up to an unacceptably high level. No; this in itself is not the answer. And it is certainly not the answer for the firm to adopt a 'mañana' attitude to estate work; such an attitude, if persisted in over a period, is liable to do considerable damage to any reputation which the firm may have for reliability. Although many firms may be loath to believe it, lay people can be very understanding when the facts are properly explained to them, and a clear indication that an unforeseeable log-jam has arisen, coupled with an offer, in an appropriate case, to enlist outside help, is far better than a succession of broken promises each of which increases the victim's exasperation.

Another matter worthy of mention is that in some quarters there is a deep-rooted practice of referring to all deceased estates as 'probates'. Now it is undeniable that, where a grant of probate is required, obtaining it is an important part of the job. But it is not the whole job, nor even the objective. To put it in its proper perspective it is a task on the way to the objective, which is to get the estate into the hands of the people who are entitled to it. To call an estate a probate tends to obscure this objective and create a psychological barrier, so that once the grant of probate has been obtained the main work is regarded as having been done, and the remaining functions of collecting the assets, meeting the commitments, preparing accounts and distributing the estate funds are regarded as matters of minor significance. This sort of approach simply will not do.

In a book of this type, which is intended for *all* to read, whether familiar with technical terms or not, some simplification is necessary in the interests of clarity. In particular there are four expressions which are used in this book and ought to be explained. They are:

Executor. In strictness this means a person appointed by a will (or by a codicil, which is a supplementary will) to carry out the wishes of the deceased person. In this book the term is used to mean the person who is actually handling the estate, who may be an executor in the strict sense, or may be an administrator (who is officially appointed in the absence of an available executor) or a professional adviser, clerk, bank official or even a kind friend who happens to own a typewriter. Where, exceptionally, the word 'executor' is used in its strict sense, this will be made clear.

The Relatives are the beneficiaries, that is the persons who are entitled to the estate under the will or, if there is no effective will, under the law. Usually the persons so entitled are relatives but they could be friends or charities. Even the State can be the beneficiary in some circumstances; in that case its own officials would normally handle the estate, but if the deceased person had outlived all his relatives, and if all the persons named in his will (except his executor) were also dead, it would then be incumbent on the executor, if he wished to act, to administer the estate for the State.

Grant means a grant of representation, i.e. probate or letters of administration, obtained from a probate registry.

Duty Threshold is the lowest level at which the death duty, which is currently called Inheritance Tax, is payable on an estate. At this time (Jan 1987), Duty Threshold is £71,000 but this is liable to change and should be checked before applying the Duty Threshold to a particular estate. Sometimes, in order to decide whether the estate reaches the Duty Threshold, it may be necessary to count in with the estate any lifetime gifts made by the deceased, and perhaps any trust funds in which the deceased was interested, but any reader who wishes to go into greater detail about this should refer to a specialised (and up-to-date) book about Inheritance Tax, which was formerly known as Capital Transfer Tax.

Chapter 2

INFORMATION

Let us begin by stating the obvious. Before the executor can take effective steps of any kind he needs facts. If it falls to him to arrange the funeral he needs facts to enable him first to register the death. And when he comes to grips with his main job of administering the estate he needs a great many more facts. Basically these centre on what the deceased owned ('assets') and owed ('liabilities'). The funeral expenses, though incurred after death, count as liabilities of the estate.

It is at this very earliest stage, the stage of assembling the facts, that scope for inefficiency first creeps in. Even if the estate is fairly small, many points must be looked into if the requirements of officialdom are to be met with the minimum of trouble and delay. An efficient executor who is intent on making rapid progress will use some kind of reminder form or checklist of which an example appears in Appendix A. If he prefers to rely on memory he is almost certain to overlook something and it is very probable that his oversight will not come to light until he is filling in the official forms, so that work on them will have to be stopped while he pursues his further enquiries. For instance, it may be necessary, depending on circumstances, to obtain information about lifetime gifts made by the deceased person, and the need for this information is something which can be, and often is, overlooked in the absence of some form of reminder. Another oversight, which can be disastrous, is to make a list of the debts which the deceased owed without giving a thought to the possibility that he might have given guarantees, perhaps in connection with someone else's bank account. And the bank or other creditor may come on the scene with a claim just when the estate has reached an advanced stage and the relatives are expecting their money.

Normally the first step in assembling the information is to read the deceased's papers and perhaps ask some questions. Letter-writing comes later when the executor has gained some idea of what assets and liabilities there may be and what gaps there are in his information. A competent executor with a good general knowledge of business matters can elicit a great deal from the papers and save time and trouble later. But it is important to look at all available documents and papers; if some of the papers are held, for example, by a bank, and the executor does not bother to go through them, some unpleasant surprises may be in store.

Usually there comes a stage at which all the assets and liabilities have been identified even though their exact amounts or values at the date of death may not yet be known. At this stage it may be possible, by the use of intelligent approximations, to say whether the estate, along with any lifetime gifts and trust funds which may have to be counted in with it, can possibly reach the Duty Threshold. If it is quite clear that that threshold cannot be reached, then it may be possible to speed up the whole operation by cutting down the amount of letter-writing at this stage or even dispensing with it entirely.

Let us take an example. Having read the deceased's papers and asked the right questions our executor is satisfied that there are no lifetime gifts or trust funds to be counted in ('aggregated') and that the estate will consist of:

1. Small house, mortgaged to a building society;
2. Household and personal belongings ('chattels');
3. Cash found in the house, £17.33;
4. Current account at a local branch bank;
5. Deposit account at the same branch bank;
6. National Savings Bank account;
7. National Savings Certificates;
8. Three small life assurance policies, not pledged to the building society;
9. Two small shareholdings in quoted companies;
10. Balance of salary to death;
11. An income tax repayment.

The liabilities are:
A. The funeral account;
B. The building society mortgage;
C. A telephone bill.

Among the deceased's papers are a statement from the building society showing the last annual balance, struck several months ago; recent statements of the current and deposit accounts; cheque stubs and paying-in counterfoils; the savings bank passbook and savings certificate books; the life policies and some bonus notices; the two share certificates; various payslips including that for the last month-end before death; a notice from the tax office; the telephone bill, and a renewal receipt for the last premium on the chattels insurance. The deeds of the house are not with the papers because of course the building society holds them as security.

This set of circumstances, though imaginary, is not untypical. As might be expected in a case in which the house is still mortgaged, the bank balances are small and so is the holding of savings certificates. The net estate (assets less liabilities) looks unlikely to come within £20,000 of the Duty Threshold. Without giving any further thought to that aspect of the matter, the executor sends out a batch of routine letters. They are addressed to:

1. A property valuer, asking him to value the house at the date of death;
2. A chattel auctioneer, asking him to value the contents of the house at that date;
3. The local bank, for statements of the two accounts;
4. The National Savings Bank, for the balance at the date of death;
5. The Savings Certificate Division, for a valuation of the certificates at the date of death;
6. The life office, for the amounts payable under the three policies;
7. A firm of stockbrokers, for a valuation of the shares;
8. The deceased's employers, for details of the salary outstanding;
9. The tax office, for a claim form;
10. The undertaker, for his account;
11. The building society, for the balance owing at death;
12. British Telecom, for confirmation of the amount of the telephone bill.

Now out of twelve letters of this kind it is likely that seven or eight will be answered fairly promptly and therefore that most of the required information will have arrived within a few days. The rest will come trickling in over two or three weeks, having been delayed by holidays, strikes, overwork, problems in transit and so on.

Well then, what does the executor do next, and when?

It is just possible that, before the letters went off, he listed them so that, by ticking off the replies instead of having to wade through his carbon copies, he would know when all the replies were in and progress was possible. It is conceivable that he may even have given some thought to the matter when the bulk of the replies arrived; perhaps he wondered whether the outstanding ones were important enough to justify waiting. But it is more likely that he will have left the replies to come in unmonitored and that the arrival of the last one will have passed unnoticed. In that case, nothing more may be done about the estate until something or someone rouses the executor into action.

Which is bad. But not unusual.

The theme of this book is delay, a potential cause of which has just been described. In this instance it might have been avoided by monitoring the incoming replies or by making a diary note (or some other reminder) to review on a given date. But it is pertinent to ask whether, in the circumstances, the letters need have been written at all.

The executor's need to put values on all the assets arises from his duty to account to the relatives and the Inland Revenue. At such an early stage in the administration of the estate it is hardly likely that the relatives would be pressing him for accounts or for anything more than approximations. And as the estate falls below the Duty Threshold by a very large margin it is certainly unlikely that the Revenue would be insisting on meticulous accuracy. As it happens they could not have such accuracy in any case, because the most significant asset is the house, and a house, unlike a bank balance, cannot be valued to the last penny on a given day. Its value is a matter of opinion, and it follows that if one item in the estate is estimated, then the total itself is only approximate. So it would have been sensible if the executor had asked himself what was at stake before writing his twelve letters. The current and deposit accounts could have been approximated from the information available (statements and cheque stubs and paying-in vouchers); the National Savings Bank balance and Savings Certificate values could have been calculated from published information about interest rates; the policies and bonus notices could have been studied to ascertain the amounts payable; the shares could probably have been valued with sufficient accuracy from quotations published in a newspaper; the salary to the date of death could have been arrived at from the last month's payslip; the tax claim could have been worked out from the deceased's known income to date of death and the tax paid on it; the undertaker could have been telephoned for the amount of his bill; and the building society balance could have been taken from the statement available and adjusted for monthly instalments paid since. As to the house and contents, these could have been put in at fairly high values without detriment. '*Could have been*' is the common theme. Well, why not? The estate papers could have been drawn up without any delay whatever.

Obviously one would not advocate a short cut of this kind if it entailed a disproportionate amount of trouble and risk. But tolerances are there to be used, and if the net estate is well under the Duty Threshold and the total is bound to depend on estimated figures anyway (in this case the values of the house and contents) there is no point in delaying the whole operation in order to ensure that the remaining assets and liabilities are exact to the last penny.

In some cases even the Duty Threshold is irrelevant; if the estate is exempt from Inheritance Tax (for instance, if the deceased's husband or wife is entitled to the whole estate) then it is even more pointless to delay the procedures while exact figures are compiled. The matter of exemptions is dealt with more fully in Chapter 5.

Chapter 3

ANTICIPATION — THE KEY TO PROGRESS

Having assembled all the facts which are required for making progress, the executor needs to think. In particular he needs to anticipate events. Anticipation is the key to getting the estate work done smoothly and quickly. Perhaps at this juncture it should be said that there are some professional executors who, as a matter of policy, refuse to take any step until it becomes necessary. Their reasoning is that if, in the long run, a step which they have taken proves to be unnecessary they will not be able to charge the estate for it and will have wasted their valuable professional time. For the moment it is sufficient to place on record that this point of view exists; it will be disregarded so far as this chapter is concerned but will be dealt with on its merits in the chapter on professional executors.

The questions to which the executor's mind should be addressed are:

1. Is a grant necessary? If it is,
    (a) how many copies of it will be required?
    (b) is it necessary to file an Inland Revenue account?
2. Are there any foreseeable problems relating to Inheritance Tax?
3. Are there any foreseeable problems relating to other taxation?
4. Would it be prudent to advertise for claims against the estate?
5. Are any of the relatives missing?
6. Which assets will be sold and which retained?
7. Who will draw up the estate accounts?
8. What arrangements are to be made to prevent the file of estate papers (perhaps very voluminous) from falling into disarray?

All these are matters, and there may be others arising in

individual cases, which are highly relevant to the time factor in estate administration. Failure to take timely action can result in delay which may well be prolonged. And each of these matters is important enough to merit a separate chapter of this book.

It has to be accepted that there are many people who cannot anticipate anything and can only get through their affairs by taking everything as it comes. No doubt such people can be very conscientious if faced with the duties of executorship, but it is hardly likely that their work will be expeditious.

On the other hand there must also be many people who would gladly reap the benefit of working to an estate programme if only they knew how to compile one. The trouble here is that no two estates are exactly alike and it is therefore impossible to write an omnibus programme which would suit them all. However, Appendix B contains an Estate Administration Checklist which, it is hoped, will help in this respect. As it stands the checklist is not suitable for use as an estate programme, but by selecting the items relevant to a particular estate and amplifying them as necessary a workable programme can be quickly written or dictated.

For instance, items about boats and caravans will not be required if the deceased did not leave a boat or caravan; and if he had several bank accounts they will all be specified by name. Again, the post-grant step of registering copies with banks and others will be enlarged to specify the actual registrations necessary in the particular case. And so on, throughout the list, the idea being to specify, as far as possible, everything which will have to be done throughout the whole administration of the estate. Obviously unforeseen developments are liable to occur, such as the belated discovery of further assets, and these developments will have to be dealt with; but the mere fact that the programme may have to be adapted to accommodate changes of this kind does not destroy the case for having a programme at all. A great deal of thinking and working time can be saved if one can work from a programme instead of having to wade through the file whenever any action is necessary.

Chapter 4

THE GRANT

Ignoring technicalities, the grant is the document which in the normal case enables the executor to collect the assets. To appreciate its significance, let us imagine that an executor, following the death of his aunt, goes to her bank and says:

"I am my aunt's executor; please let me have her money."

The bank official's reply is likely to be

"Certainly, if you will let us have official proof that you are entitled to it."

So the executor, or his solicitor, fills in the prescribed forms and submits them to a probate registry with the will and the probate fees and Inheritance Tax (if any) and after a few days the executor receives a piece of paper naming him as the person authorised to deal with the estate. This is the grant; and as there is a will a neat photocopy of it will be attached to the grant. Having thus obtained the grant the executor takes or sends it to the bank and, subject perhaps to satisfying the bank that he is the person named as executor in the grant, receives his aunt's money.

Now the instance which has just been mentioned is an obvious case in which a grant is necessary. But there are equally obvious cases in which it is not. Let us suppose that the aunt's estate consisted entirely of personal belongings and cash under the floorboards. Clearly the executor could take possession of these without the need for an official piece of paper. And some people have all their investments and bank accounts standing in the names of others (nominees) and here again there is no need for a grant. But where the estate is large enough to be charged with Inheritance Tax the Revenue will insist on an account even if there is no grant.

A further exception to the need for a grant arises in certain cases in which, under regulations, it is possible to collect assets (e.g. National Savings and small insurance policies) without a grant. But sometimes the advantage of doing so is more apparent than real. If a large number of relatives will share in the estate, and a single form of consent has to be sent to all of them for signature before the money can be paid, it may be quicker and easier to apply for a grant than to try to collect without one. So the real question is whether the assets can be collected more expeditiously with or without a grant.

Let us assume that it has been decided in the case of an estate that a grant is required. The grant is applied for and obtained, but it is a single document, and if it has to be sent to ten or more different places, as in the case of the imaginary estate in Chapter 2, it will be a very long time before all the assets become available to the executor even if the grant is not lost somewhere on its way round. To an efficient executor this is no problem; before he lodges his application for a grant he will count the number of places to which it has to go and when he applies for his grant he will order sufficient 'office copies' to enable all the assets to be dealt with at the same time. The office copies are official photocopies of the grant, each bearing an embossed device as a sign of authenticity, and they are accepted as valid instead of the grant itself.

While he is waiting for the grant and office copies to arrive from the registry our efficient executor will prepare the covering letters (if any are necessary) and the documents, such as share certificates or passbooks, which will be sent for 'registration', as the process is called. Covering letters may not be strictly necessary if there is nothing to say when office copies and documents are sent for registration; but if, as suggested in Chapter 2, assets have been approximated as at the date of death, then it is a good idea when sending the papers for registration to ask for confirmation of the exact figure so that it will subsequently be available for accounting purposes. If the executor knows at this stage whether assets are to be sold or retained he may, in his covering letter, ask for the appropriate forms (e.g. for National Savings) if, indeed, he has not obtained them already. And while on the subject of registration it is worth noting that the Inspector of Taxes likes to know what is happening to the estate, so that if the original grant has a copy will attached to it that original should be sent to the Inspector rather than an office copy.

In some quarters office copies, though not actually taboo, are only ordered in very small numbers which means that all the registrations cannot be done at once. For instance, three copies may be ordered to cover twelve registrations, the idea being to save expense. This is a false economy; it means not only that there will be delay in completing the registrations but also that a strict control has to be maintained so that, at any given time, it is known where the copies have already been sent and where they have still to go. The cost of this time-consuming and tedious chore far outweighs the cost of the extra office copies. On the other hand, if there is no monitoring at all of the documents sent for registration the estate may lapse into inactivity until someone jogs the executor's memory. The possibility of this happening has already been mentioned, as regards information letters, in Chapter 2. Either a checklist should be kept (and ticked as the letters come in) or a suitable diary note or other reminder should be made.

When sending copies of the grant for registration the executor must expect the arrival, in reply, of a large volume of paper. It is the practice of some companies to send forms (e.g. dividend mandates) without being asked, so suitable arrangements should be made to weed out the unwanted forms as they arrive, in order to avoid later confusion about which forms are wanted and the possibility that time may be wasted in filling in the wrong ones in error.

Chapter 5

INHERITANCE TAX

As we saw in Chapter 1, the Duty Threshold is changed from time to time but is at Jan 1987 £71,000. Requirements of the Inland Revenue also change in matters of detail, but broadly speaking estates may be regarded as falling into three categories for accounting purposes, namely:

1. Those above the Duty Threshold. In these cases an account of the estate has to be filed and normally the tax has to be paid (if payable at all) before the grant is issued, even if this involves, as it frequently does, obtaining a bank loan;
2. Those below the Duty Threshold on which tax is not payable but for which the filing of an account is still required;
3. Very small estates on which no tax is payable and for which no account has to be filed.

The vast majority of estates fall into categories 2 and 3, and usually no problem arises. But in any case in which there may have to be negotiations about values — i.e. in category I. and perhaps the top part of 2. — the competent executor will identify the areas likely to come under scrutiny and equip himself to deal with them. If he does nothing until he receives a set of queries from the Capital Taxes Office of the Inland Revenue the subsequent negotiations, if protracted, may well delay the closing of the estate. Some assets, such as bank balances, can be readily quantified and are unlikely to give rise to protracted negotiations. Others cannot, and a frequent cause of difficulty and delay is the valuation of shareholdings in unquoted companies. Very often in order to save time the grant is applied for before all the details normally required (e.g. balance sheets) have come to hand and, while there is no harm in this, the executor should at least find out, as soon as he can, where the sources of information are so that he will be able to tap them when necessary. Very often the source of information about an unquoted company's affairs is the office of an accountant or professional secretary far removed from the company's place of business. Another problem area is the checking of Inheritance Tax assessments in cases in which there are aggregable assets — say trust funds and lifetime gifts — which have to be counted in with the estate for calculation purposes. The situation is further complicated if, let us say, some assets are exempt, some are taxable by instalments and the rest are taxable in a lump sum in the ordinary way. In all these cases the assessments follow a definite pattern which can, however, be extremely confusing to those who are not familiar with it. This is not a problem which will go away; if the executor cannot understand the assessments sufficiently to be able to check them properly he should seek competent advice. Otherwise he may still be arguing about assessments when he should be closing the estate.

Before leaving the subject of Inheritance Tax it is opportune to mention that the tax does not apply universally. As we have seen, small estates are exempt and so, normally, is property left to a surviving spouse. But exemptions may apply to other classes of property. The rules are complex and cannot be given in detail here, but a list of headings under which exemptions may fall is given below so that, in appropriate cases, the reader may be alerted to the possibility of exemption and consequently to the need to refer to a more specialised work on the subject:

1. Property of someone who has died on active service;
2. Property outside the United Kingdom, the deceased having been domiciled outside the United Kingdom;
3. A reversionary interest (i.e. one which will come to a person on the happening of some event) but not one purchased by the deceased or a previous owner;
4. A dependant's annuity under an approved contract or trust scheme (the reasoning here is that if the deceased opted to have the annuity paid to the dependant instead of having a lump sum paid to his estate it would be unreasonable to regard the lump sum as his anyway);
5. Certain government annuities in foreign ownership;
6. Certain overseas pensions;
7. Certain savings (e.g. National Savings) where the deceased was domiciled in the Channel Islands or Isle of Man;
8. Property of visiting forces and allied headquarters staffs;
9. Property passing on the death of a surviving spouse who only had a life interest in it as from the first spouse's death (but the exemption only applies where estate duty — the death duty which preceded the introduction of the

tax now known as Inheritance Tax — was paid on the property on that first death);
10. Property left to certain specified bodies concerned with national purposes;
11. Property (within limits) left to charities or political parties;
12. Land, buildings or articles left for the public benefit, subject to conditions.

Quite apart from the categories listed above, as being possibly applicable to the deceased's estate on death, lifetime gifts made by the deceased should be considered to see whether they fall within exemptions allowed by law. But no useful purpose can be served by continuing such an exercise if the whole estate is exempt from tax anyway.

Chapter 6

INCOME TAX AND CAPITAL GAINS TAX

One of the standard excuses given by an executor who is being pressed by relatives to divide the estate is "I'm waiting for the tax man." Probably this is true; it is not by any means unusual for the closing of the estate to be held up by income tax problems. But the executor may only have told part of the story. When did he start his dealings with the tax office? After all the rest of the estate work had been done? Tax work is something which an executor who lacks numeracy detests and which tends to be put off until it can be deferred no longer. Yet it can often be a more protracted job than anything else connected with the estate.

Another approach which is hardly to be recommended is to muddle through the estate tax work without any clear idea of what is happening, relying on the tax inspector (who may himself be working on incomplete information) to get matters right. If an assessment for, say, £250 arrives the executor pays £250 out of the estate funds and hopes that that will be the end of the matter. It may not be, of course; further assessments may come in after the executor has paid out all the estate to the relatives.

The diligent executor will address his mind to the tax aspects of the estate as soon as the deceased's assets and liabilities have been identified. He will draw a clear distinction between

(a) the deceased's own tax position at the date of death and
(b) the taxable income of the estate during administration.

Nothing can be done about the latter until it arises, but the former is an asset or liability of the estate at the date of death, depending on whether the deceased had overpaid or underpaid tax to that date. If it is clear from the start that the deceased did not pay any tax and was not liable for any, then there is no problem. Or the deceased may have had a tax adviser who handled his affairs and is prepared (quickly?) to sort out the position at the date of death. In these days of electronics calculations should not give rise to prolonged delays. Negotiations may; but if the tax adviser envisages difficulties in arriving at an accurate figure the executor should be apprised of the issues and given a provisional figure subject to later adjustment if necessary. If, of course, decisions have to be made (e.g. whether to adopt a particular course acceptable to the Inspector of Taxes) these decisions should be made by the executor, not the tax adviser. The executor is entitled to avail himself of the adviser's expertise but should remain in control.

Frequently, however, there is no tax adviser and it is not even clear whether any tax element is involved. If the current position cannot be gathered from the deceased's papers the executor should without delay contact the appropriate Inspector of Taxes to obtain a copy of the deceased's last tax return. Sometimes this copy return discloses assets or sources of income of which the executor was previously unaware, and the possibility of such disclosures is in itself, regardless of other considerations, a good reason for making contact with the tax office at an early stage.

If there is any difficulty in ascertaining the address of the correct tax office, and there is no mention of this in the deceased's papers, the last employer may be able to help or, if the deceased was not employed, a tax office in the district (for which see the local telephone directory). If all these approaches fail, the Board of Inland Revenue is at Somerset House, London WC2. But do not allow these preliminaries (i.e. sorting out the right tax office) to get bogged down. The real tax issues remain to be dealt with and may hold up the estate work unless they are started early. And if a new tax adviser has to be called in to achieve progress, it is clearly unsatisfactory (although it does happen) that the newcomer should be someone who is himself unable to find time to deal with the job. This state of affairs can hold up an estate for months or even years.

Usually estate tax problems tend to centre on income tax rather than capital gains tax. This is because death is not treated as a 'disposal' for capital gains tax purposes, so that the deceased's capital gains are not taxed unless realised before death.

The foregoing observations apply to the tax position at death. During the period of administration proper records should be kept of taxed and untaxed income received by the estate and of realised capital gains. In due course the executor will be asked to make a return of the estate income, if it is significant for tax purposes, and, if the income is divided up, a trust income statement showing how much income each of the relatives (as distinct from the estate as a whole) has received and how much tax has been paid by deduction.

Sometimes the estate involves a discretionary trust, for which the tax returns and calculations can be daunting for those who are unfamiliar with the practice. One can only advise an executor to seek assistance with the forms if he finds them incomprehensible. Nothing will be achieved by ignoring them.

Chapter 7
ADVERTISING FOR CLAIMS

It is for the executor to decide whether he should avail himself of the protection afforded by Section 27 Trustee Act 1925, under which he can give notice by advertisement to creditors and others having claims against, or interests in, the estate to send them in by a certain date. When the date has passed, the estate may be safely distributed without making provision for claims not sent in. But this statement is subject to several reservations.

In the first place, the executor must not ignore a claim actually known to him even if the claimant does not answer the advertisement.

Secondly, it is not sufficient to advertise in the prescribed papers (i.e. the London Gazette and a newspaper circulating in a district where the estate owns land) if there is any reason to think that there may be claimants in another country.

And finally, but quite importantly, the protection given to the executor does not prevent the claimant from pursuing his claim after the estate has been distributed. In that case the claim is presented to the relatives who have received the estate. But suppose the executor is himself solely entitled to the estate — is the protection of any value to him? This is something which he must decide.

The aspect of the matter with which this book is mainly concerned is that the advertised date (meaning the date by which the claims have to be in) must be at least two months after the day on which the advertisement appears. For this reason it is important that the executor should make an early decision whether to advertise. If he does nothing about it until he is ready to divide the estate, and then gets cold feet and decides to advertise, he will need to hold on to at least some of the assets until the two-month period has expired. And this will entail a further decision which would not have been necessary if he had acted sooner — how much of the estate is to be kept back?

It is opportune in this connection to mention the subject of partial distributions. A partial distribution is a sensible way of dealing with the situation where it is impossible to pay out the whole estate because of outstanding claims, actual or potential. Relatives tend to be furious, and with some justification, if an unnecessarily large fund is being withheld from them as cover for comparatively small claims. On the other hand the executor cannot be blamed for erring on the side of caution, especially if any of the claims are of uncertain amount, but if a significant fund has to be kept in hand he should keep it on deposit as long as possible and keep the relatives informed about what is happening.

Chapter 8

MISSING RELATIVES

If the estate has to be divided equally among the deceased's eight children and the executor only knows the whereabouts of two of them, then the shares of the remaining six (three quarters of the entire fund) cannot be distributed until those six are accounted for satisfactorily.

And it is obvious that if the executor takes no steps to trace the missing six until he is ready, in all other ways, to divide the estate, the process of division will be needlessly prolonged. So the sooner he starts to look for them the better.

The following suggestions may help:

(a) A letter to a former address is sometimes worth while, because even if the missing one is known to have left it, some form of redirection may be in operation.
(b) If the missing person has lived or expressed a wish to live in a particular area, reference may be made to the telephone directory for that area.
(c) No harm is done by ringing a likely telephone number. If, as a result, the executor is asked to state his business, he can say that he wishes to account for a small sum of money without (unless he is sure he is on to the right person) saying how much.
(d) Did the missing person belong to a club, association, trade union, etc? The secretary may know where he is.
(e) Are there any friends or relatives who may have recent news?
(f) Ex-employers may be in touch with, and may even be paying a pension to, the person sought.
(g) If the person was ever in the armed forces, service records may help.
(h) A complaint requiring regular treatment may point to residence near a suitably-equipped hospital or clinic.

Obviously the lines of enquiry must depend on circumstances, but it is quite likely that at some stage a person (such as a club secretary) will be found who knows the missing person's address but refuses to divulge it. This is understandable, and in such a case it is a good idea to ask the person concerned to forward a letter. This is not the same thing as divulging the address; the addressee need not answer unless he wishes. But the letter thus sent should be sufficiently explicit to induce the addressee to answer.

It is comparatively unusual for all the leads to fail if they are properly followed up. If they do fail, it may be time to consider the possibility that the information on which the executor has been working may be wrong. It is by no means unknown for relatives to state quite emphatically that the missing member of the family is, say, Bill, whereas in fact (and perhaps unknown to them) Bill's birth was registered as Tom, under which name he is living happily somewhere, having forgotten that anyone ever called him Bill. So if promising leads fail, the next stage is to get down to fundamentals and try to get the missing person's correct name and as much further detail as possible. A birth certificate, if obtainable, is a useful document in a search of this kind.

If all the leads still fail it may be necessary to advertise. Should this be so, it is important to ensure that prominence is given to the name of the person sought rather than the name of the deceased. For instance, if the person sought is Mrs. Ann Smith, daughter of Mr. John Brown (deceased) and niece of Mrs. Jane Robinson (whose estate is being administered and has given rise to the need to trace Mrs. Smith) it is Mrs. Smith's name which should stand out and not, as is so often the case with many conventional forms of notice, the names of the two deceased persons. The reason for this is that it is quite likely that Mrs. Smith may not read the notice herself but may be told of it by local busybodies who have recognised her name. Busybodies can be useful people when missing persons are being hunted out, and their assistance should not be spurned. A further point is that the advertisement should indicate, if only in general terms, the reason why Mrs. Smith is wanted.

If advertising brings no result it is not unreasonable to consider the possibility that the missing person may be dead. Armed with the information about the unsuccessful efforts to trace him, it may be possible to insure against the possibility of his appearing on the scene after his share has been paid out to other people on the assumption that he is dead.

But all these things take time, and that time does not have to run from the day on which the estate is ready for distribution. A wise executor will have started his enquiries soon after entering on his duties.

Chapter 9

ASSETS — SELL OR KEEP?

It is an unfortunate fact that many deceased estates lie dormant for a long period after the grant has been obtained and registered. By then a great mass of paper may have accumulated, as not only will the office copies of the grant have come back (each marked to show where it has been, rather on the lines of windscreen stickers on cars) but they will have been accompanied by a fine collection of acknowledgments, claim forms, receipts, dividend mandate forms and other printed matter for the executor's attention.

The reasons for the tendency towards inactivity are not far to seek. Not only does it require courage to tackle the mass of paperwork, but the underlying situation which the mass of papers indicate is quite different from anything else which has happened since the deceased died. Up to now it has been possible, admittedly by jettisoning efficiency, to do practically everything in an automatic, mindless way. But now it is necessary to think. To think, that is, about how the debts and funeral expenses are to be paid; about how much will be necessary to meet pecuniary legacies (i.e. sums of money) and the expenses of executorship; about professional fees, provision for tax, and so on. And having arrived at a total for these, to decide which assets are to be sold now to cover them, and which are to be sold later in the hope of an improved market, and which are to be transferred to the relatives in kind. (Incidentally, the expression 'in specie', which is often used instead of 'in kind', really means in coin as distinct from paper money.)

It has long been recognised that executors are entitled to employ and pay stockbrokers, bankers, solicitors and others and at this stage of the administration it is often useful to have some expert advice. But on what? It is unlikely that the answers will be right if the wrong questions are asked. So, taking the matter step by step:

1. How much money is needed to meet all commitments?
2. How much of that is available already?

3. What assets can be realised to cover the balance?
4. Need they all be realised at once, or can some sales be deferred (e.g. to cover expenses not yet incurred or tax not yet assessed)?

With these questions answered the executor can discuss with his advisers the sales necessary to provide £x as soon as possible and £y at a later stage. In this connection it should not be overlooked that if Inheritance Tax is being paid by instalments and the properties (or some of them) on which the instalments are payable are sold, all the remaining instalments on those properties will become payable at once and can no longer be spread over the years.

In all these operations the executor is the central figure. Unless he uses his authority to keep matters moving they are likely to grind to a halt, despite increasing clamour from the (still unpaid) undertaker.

Chapter 10

ESTATE ACCOUNTS

This, like taxation, is an area in which executors who are not numerate find themselves floundering. What is liable to happen is that the long-suffering relatives have to press for an account and when they get it they find that it is virtually a copy of the estate bank statement, finishing up with the present bank balance as the amount available for distribution. Items of capital and income are there, all mixed up, in the order in which they were received or paid; proceeds of insurances are well concealed among dividends, rents and sales of shares so that the relatives cannot, without spending hours on analysis, get any sort of idea of what is really happening. Assets which have not given rise to any cash transactions, such as unsold shares, properties, furniture and jewellery, are not featured at all; nor are commitments which have not yet been met. "There's no need to mention the income tax; we've still got property which should more than cover it." So goes the explanation of the shortcomings.

If estate accounts are to be adequate they should show clearly:

1. The estate capital, consisting of the assets at death (all of them, whether since sold or not) less the deceased's debts and funeral expenses;
2. Income during the administration of the estate;
3. Administration expenses, including Inheritance Tax;
4. The balance available for the relatives, after allowing for commitments not yet met;
5. The distribution of that balance among the relatives, which should tie up with the will or the law of intestacy.

Usually the accounts are divided into sections, corresponding roughly with the numbered categories above, but this is not an inflexible rule. For instance, it is rather pointless to have a folio headed 'Income Account' if there is only one item of income. And there is no need to have elaborate appropriation and distribution accounts if, without further complication, the whole of the capital and income belong, after meeting commitments, to one person.

Clarity rather than formality should be the keynote. If the executor is not clear about what he is doing he should not try to prepare the accounts himself. His best service to the relatives is to find a competent professional who will draw up the accounts clearly and quickly.

Chapter 11

PAPERS IN DISARRAY

It is impossible to administer an estate without papers. The trouble is that they are liable to get completely out of control, and when this happens the executor does not know what work he has still to do or who is entitled to what. Estate papers are of many kinds, and they refuse to conform to any pattern as regards shape and size.

Probably the most useful filing folder for general estate work is the type with a single pocket and a file fitting opposite. With this the correspondence, punched, can be kept in order of date on the file fitting and the motley collection of other papers can go in the pocket. These papers in the pocket will, however, tend to drop out and get lost when the file is handled in the course of normal use. Probably the best way of coping with this is to keep them in transparent plastic bags or folders within the pocket. The deceased's own papers, required for reference, are not part of the general estate correspondence and it is suggested that they also be kept in the pocket in a separate transparent plastic bag or folder. It remains to decide what papers constitute 'correspondence', to be punched and filed, and probably the most convenient place to draw the line is to treat as correspondence not only the letters but all the papers (e.g. certificates of balance) which will not be required for further processing. Papers which *will* be required for further processing include forms to be completed and signed, bank statements to be kept together, dividend counterfoils to accompany the tax return, and so on. All these will go in the pocket. The filing fitting will only contain papers which will not foreseeably have to be removed from the file.

This suggestion, of course, is meant to cover estates of average size and complexity. For a very small or very simple estate, consisting perhaps of one bank account, it may not be necessary to acquire any filing equipment at all. And for a very large and complex one the suggested folder might be insufficient; it might be better to use box files or wallets with double pockets or cloth gussets. But the general principle remains whether the estate is large or small; correspondence is filed chronologically and other papers are kept as conveniently as possible until they are required. Documents of title, such as share certificates or deeds of property, are best kept under lock and key in some safe place. And it is not a good idea to keep each share certificate in a separate envelope; this impedes access to the certificates when needed. Far better is the system of keeping all the certificates firmly clipped together in alphabetical order of company names with, perhaps, government stock certificates on top. In this way the certificates can be easily referred to and easily removed.

But how is filing connected with delay? Anyone who has ever had to face a huge mound of estate papers, with letters, deeds, share certificates, forms, uncashed cheques and warrants (some of them old enough to require renewal) and even cash, all piled up together, knows the sheer impossibility of making rapid progress when nothing can be found.

Chapter 12

PROFESSIONAL EXECUTORS

Executorship is a job which calls for a number of different skills and aptitudes. In the early stages of administering an estate the executor may need to be something of a detective, working from incomplete information to find out what the deceased actually left. He also needs to be something of an administrator, lawyer, accountant and diplomat. He has to have a wide knowledge of commercial matters if he is to deal successfully with bank accounts, insurances, stocks and shares. Ideally he will have the patience to wait while normal procedures go through their channels but the ability to force the pace when something is taking too long.

In fact he will be a rather ideal sort of person!

As there are few people who have all the necessary skills and aptitudes it is likely that at some stage professional help will be sought. Maybe the whole job of handling the estate will be entrusted to a specialist in executorship.

What, then, is likely to happen, and why are there so many complaints about delay?

As in any other field of human activity there are good and bad. At one end of the spectrum, an estate may be entrusted to a highly efficient person who, if lacking in some of the requisite skills, has the intelligence to seek them elsewhere and keep the operation moving at an acceptable rate. At the other end, the job may be handled by someone who, perhaps due to inadequate training, wastes time going through unnecessary procedures and, while giving every outward appearance of being busy, is in reality achieving nothing. The routine character of much of the work of administering an estate tends to lead to task-orientation, i.e. seeing the job in terms of what is done ('writing letters') rather than in terms of what is achieved ('getting people their money without delay'). Examples of this include:

1. Spending a whole morning putting share certificates into separate foolscap envelopes and writing on each envelope (perhaps in very beautiful handwriting) the details of the

certificate within. This is a sheer waste of time and envelopes. Nothing has been achieved by the morning's work; the certificates are less accessible than they were before and will have to be taken out of the envelopes when they are needed. Even checking that the right certificates are still there will entail removal from the envelopes.

2. Drafting an over-formal set of accounts. Mention has already been made in Chapter 10 of the inadequacy of some accounts which are merely a re-hash of the bank statements. That is an example of not taking enough trouble to prepare proper accounts; likewise it is possible to take too much. Let us suppose that an estate has one freehold property, one quoted investment, one unquoted investment, one bank account, one insurance policy and one building society account. The task oriented clerk, obsessed with the idea that different assets should be separately scheduled, prepares six one-page schedules, each containing one entry, and carries the six items into the main account.

3. Abandoning the file in an unfinished state when the clerk has carried out all the routine tasks and has reached a point at which he is out of his depth. Sometimes, perhaps not by accident, the abandoned file does not come to light until the person concerned has moved on to another place of employment.

It must be stressed that, although all these things actually happen, they are not the norm, and in general professional executors handle their work competently. Obviously the cases described above indicate failure to train and/or control the employee properly. In each case the unintelligent action (or lack of action) on the part of the employee concerned would militate not only against that employee's own competitiveness as an employee but also against his employer's viability in competition with his rivals.

However, the task-oriented approach is not the only destroyer of efficiency in the professional office. Observation of many estates shows that executive time is liable to be wasted in studying files which have lain dormant for some time or have been passed from one person to another. Even in a well-ordered office it will occasionally happen that the administration of an estate has to stop for a time, perhaps until a property is sold or until finality is reached with tax negotiations, or during the absence of a relative abroad. Or the person handling the estate may leave or fall ill. In all these cases it is necessary for someone to pick up the threads when the work starts to move again, and if the files are voluminous this may take many hours or even days. And the need to pick up the threads may happen more than once if further stoppages occur in the same estate. In any event, the time spent is, from the viewpoint of the relatives, completely unproductive.

This particular problem tends to be peculiar to the professional office. An amateur executor, having only one estate to deal with, can probably keep the pattern of that estate clear in his mind and be ready to act as soon as progress becomes feasible. But the professional executor has to keep track of all the estates which he is administering and cannot rely to the same extent on his memory. The whole subject of picking up the threads is dealt with at greater length in Chapter 16.

It was stated in Chapter 3 that there were some professional executors who, as a matter of policy, refused to take any step until it became necessary, lest they might find themselves in a position of having done work for which they could not charge the estate. This appears to be a short-sighted policy, at least in relation to the suggestions for anticipating events made earlier in this book. Insofar as forward thinking is applied to operations which would have to be carried out anyway, and merely gets them done sooner, it cannot be said to be giving rise to wasted work. In fact it is difficult to envisage any situation in which intelligent anticipation could cause such waste. Unintelligent anticipation might; for instance, getting a set of share transfers ready without first finding out whether the relatives wished to sell or keep the shares. But even so, the 'no waste' advocates seem to overlook a very important consideration, which is that if, by intelligent anticipation, it becomes possible to finalise an estate in six months instead of, perhaps, eighteen, and collect the fees, then surely the resulting improvement in cash flow will outweigh any lost fees for minimal wasted work.

To sum up, the best advice to a testator who wants a professional executor, or to a lay executor who is seeking a professional adviser, must be 'Choose a good one'.

Chapter 13

SNAGS

In Chapter 3 we tried to foresee the sort of problems which might delay the closing of the estate. These problems are likely to centre on claims, perhaps for tax, or potential claims, maybe under guarantees, against the estate. It is unfair to keep the relatives waiting indefinitely for their entitlements, and yet some of the claims, if they turn on arguable technicalities, may be unquantified. It should be borne in mind, however, that however abstruse and technical the points at issue may be, they will in the end have to be settled, if valid, for money or money's worth. In the interests of the relatives it is worth going to some trouble to arrive at the maximum amount, allowing for all contingencies, which the estate could conceivably be called upon to meet (including, of course, the expense of conducting negotiations if professional advisers are involved) and setting aside a fund of that maximum amount, so that the rest of the estate is available for division among the relatives. They will also receive, in due course, any balance of the earmarked fund which may be left after settling the claims.

It is not unusual for an executor to reach the final stages of an estate with the deeds of property still on his hands — property, that is, which should be made over to the person entitled to it under the will or the intestacy laws. This operation can be carried out by a formal conveyance but more often it is done by a simple document known as an assent. If the executor is himself the person entitled to the property the assent may take the form of a short note endorsed on the last deed; otherwise, with other people involved, it will be a separate document which should preferably be prepared by someone well versed in conveyancing. If the title to the property is registered (that is, state-guaranteed) so that the executor has a title certificate instead of deeds, a printed form of assent, obtainable from a law stationer, may be found suitable. Whichever way the assenting is done, there is no reason for it to hold up dealings with the rest of the estate.

Chapter 14

COVERING UP

In the introduction we noted that executors were not overanxious to disclose their own inefficiency. Sometimes, however, this proclivity is carried a stage further, so that the executor not only fails to inform but takes positive steps to conceal. For instance, if none of the estate papers can ever be found when the relatives ask to see them it is reasonable to suppose that facts are being suppressed. And if there is a long history of 'passing the buck' by blaming the solicitor, accountant, tax inspector or some other party, there may be grounds for thinking that all is not well with the administration of the estate. At worst there may have been misappropriation but this, fortunately, is fairly unusual. It is more likely that there has been an inexcusably long spell of inactivity during which, perhaps, papers have been lost, money has been left unbanked, and current balances have not been placed on deposit. Dividend warrants and counterfoils, being small, may have been put aside on arrival and lost without trace. If estate accounts are needed, the requisite information may be impossible to assemble without a vast amount of trouble.

If the relatives have reason to think that the estate has fallen into disarray and that a deliberate cover-up is being practised, there are several steps which they may take. They can press for accounts, but these take time to prepare, and this fact may allow an incompetent executor a breathing space during which the operation may slide further into chaos. Or they may apply to a court of law to have accounts taken, in an action for the administration of the estate, and here again there is likely to be delay, though the muscle which the court can bring to bear on the executor may well prove successful in the long run. There is also machinery by which a court can remove an executor from office. But all these methods are cumbrous, and if the executor, when taken to court, succeeds in justifying his activities (or inactivities) the expenses of the court proceedings may have to be found out of the estate. Is there not a simpler approach — a means, perhaps, of testing the temperature before plunging in?

Yes, there is. It is to ask the executor a few simple questions rather than press for a set of accounts. For instance, the executor may be asked for a list of the assets which are still unadministered and of the commitments which still remain to be met. Obviously the answers to these questions will not provide as much information as would a set of accounts, but the executor's response — or lack of it — should be helpful in deciding what to do next. In a normal case, and assuming that the executor does not have work of greater urgency to do, it should be possible to provide the lists within, say, one week. However, three possibilities present themselves at this stage:

1. The executor may supply the lists as requested. If he does, and they appear to be satisfactory, it may be worth asking him to estimate how much time he needs to close the estate. Armed with the list of unadministered assets, the relatives or their advisers have the means of deciding whether the estimated period is reasonable.
2. He may reply unsatisfactorily, failing to give the information required. In this case it may be advisable to start the pressure for a full set of accounts.
3. He may not reply at all. This could mean any one of a number of things. For instance, the relatives' request may not have reached him; or he may have been too busy to deal with it; or he may be having difficulty in answering it; or he may have no intention of doing anything about it. As the relatives do not know which of these possibilities, if any, is the right one, the matter needs to be followed up. Probably the worst way of doing this is the usual "We shall be pleased to hear from you in reply to our letter of . . . " A reminder of this kind does not make the recipient think, and the reminder itself probably gets filed or thrown away. It is better to ask what is delaying the sending of the information requested, and whether they (the relatives) can help in any way. Even if it is obvious that they cannot help, this courtesy does no harm and may well make their approach look more reasonable if the issue later becomes contentious.

The principle embodied in the suggestions made in this chapter is to keep the correspondence as simple and straightforward as possible. We want a list of unadministered assets and unmet commitments. May we have one? Why not? What is the problem? How much longer must we wait for the estate to be closed?

Apropos of this principle of keeping the questions simple, the reasoning is that simple questions are less likely than complexities to drive an already bogged estate more deeply into the mire. It is a great temptation, when things are apparently going wrong, to compile a long list of difficult questions which will cause the executor to commit suicide or disappear without trace. But the object of the exercise is to get the estate moving, not to kill the executor. Compile the long list by all means, but if possible extract the information by easy stages so that there is never an entangled web which may enable the executor to justify further delay.

If, however, in the last resort the executor proves troublesome, then firmer action must be taken. It is not unknown for estates to remain open for several decades due to the failure of relatives to insist on closure. When this happens executors and relatives are liable to die before the job is completed, and the work becomes more and more difficult and expensive as time goes on.

Chapter 15

DECISIONS

In a perfect world no executor would take on an estate unless he knew that he was competent to administer it properly. In an imperfect world executors are frequently baffled and do not know which way to turn. They have not been trained in solving problems and making decisions and are perhaps unaware that such things can be done in a well-ordered way. So they just muddle through. Or perhaps they don't muddle through. They do nothing.

If the problem is a technical one and calls for skills or knowledge which the executor does not possess (e.g. solicitors', accountants' or surveyors' knowledge) then he is courting disaster if he does not get the best professional advice obtainable within the limits of the situation. But if the problem is a non-technical one and the executor must make a decision himself there may be guidelines which he can usefully follow. For instance, the following suggestions, adapted as necessary, may be useful in thinking a way through.

1. Be sure that you have identified the problem correctly. If it will help you to clear your mind, write it down.
2. Ascertain the amount at stake, expressed in money terms. A good estimate is better than nothing. Is the problem worth pursuing, or is the amount involved minimal? (It is important not to duck this part of the exercise. Sometimes a person faced with an apparent problem worries himself to the verge of a breakdown unaware that there is little or nothing to choose from when comparing, say, different courses of action.)
3. Ascertain the facts and eliminate all the irrelevant ones. This means giving due thought to what is relevant and what is not.
4. Work out possible solutions, tackling the problem methodically.
   (a) If it is complex, break it down into component subproblems and if necessary prepare a decision tree. (An example of a decision tree for settling the future

of the deceased's business, where two parties, A and B, are unequally interested in the estate, is given in Appendix C. In such a case A and B would have to concur in a solution, but the job of identifying the problems and initiating a decision would doubtless fall on the executor.)
- (b) If you are thus solving a problem by stages, do not start work on any stage until you have completed your work on the earlier stages.
- (c) If you are using a decision tree, keep the number of possibilities at each point of decision as low as possible (ideally two). If you have a great number of possibilities at any point of decision you have probably not broken the problem down far enough.
- (d) Don't follow obvious non-starters through to their logical conclusions. (The operation is not meant to be a strenuous mental exercise.)
- (e) If tolerances are available (e.g. tax thresholds or reliefs) then use them.

5. Consider the possible solutions. If there are alternatives, compare them in money terms wherever possible.
6. Reach a decision. If others have to be consulted, as in the case of the disposal of the business referred to above, consult them and give them all the facts they need to make up their minds. If the ultimate responsibility of decision is not yours, or is only partly yours, don't arrogate it to yourself, because the issues may turn on factors outside your own technical scope.

Chapter 16

PICKING UP THE THREADS

We have seen that it is not always possible for the same person to handle an estate right through from start to finish. Death, illness, change of professional adviser and other causes are liable to bring about a situation in which a newcomer to the job, with no previous knowledge of it at all, finds the papers relating to it on his desk. Suppose the estate is already in disarray. What is the new executor supposed to do? (It is convenient to continue to refer to an 'executor', as explained in Chapter 1, although it is very unlikely that the newcomer will, in strictness, be one.)

The first step is to get the papers into some sort of order. Correspondence will, of course, be sorted into order of date. Arguments will no doubt continue until the end of time as to whether the first letter should be at the front or the back of the file. This is not a matter of great moment, and the type of filing equipment which happens to be available may well dictate the decision. The important points are that the letters should be in the correct order and that they should be fastened together sufficiently firmly to stay fixed despite frequent handling. As explained in Chapter 11, papers which will not be required for further processing (i.e. which will not have to come off the file) may be treated as letters and filed accordingly.

Papers which will or may be needed for further processing (the 'may' arises because at this stage the executor will probably not know what has already been done) are best sorted in such a way that all those relating to a particular asset or liability, or a particular aspect of the work, are kept together for further attention when required.

Having put the papers into satisfactory order, the next step is to find out what assets the deceased left, and what liabilities and funeral expenses were payable. If there has been major delay this may involve going back a long way in time, but it is not normally sufficient simply to ascertain the present assets and outstanding commitments and to carry on from there. The reason is that the relatives will, in due course, want a proper account of the estate right from the beginning. There are two possible exceptions to this; in some cases the relatives may already have received and approved interim accounts, and if these are clear and satisfactory it should not be necessary to go back beyond the date to which these interim accounts were made up. Or the relatives may themselves know what remains to be done and may stipulate that nothing more is required. In the latter case, however, the taker-over risks problems; in particular, if he accepts oral assurances about the remaining assets and liabilities he may belatedly find, perhaps when he has disposed of all the assets to the relatives, that there are liabilities about which he did not know. Or there may be further assets which should have been realised and have since depreciated.

For the purpose of this book, however, it will be assumed that these two exceptions do not apply and that the executor must therefore go right back to the date of death. With the papers now in proper order it may be possible to pick up the threads quite easily. If an Inland Revenue account of the estate has been filed, and a copy of it is with the papers, it may be possible to compile from it a list of the assets and liabilities at death. (The copy account is seldom itself suitable for use as a checklist, except in very simple estates, as its layout militates against convenient reference.) If an Inland Revenue account has been filed but no copy is available it may be desirable to ask the Revenue to supply one. Quite apart from its immediate use as the basis of a checklist it is virtually certain that the copy account will be needed sooner or later in order to check the figures already supplied to the Revenue and see whether any corrections need to be made.

Once the lists have been compiled, whether from the copy Inland Revenue account or from the other papers, or from a combination of the two, it is necessary to find out what has happened since the deceased died. The usual, and probably the best, way of doing this is to start by analysing the estate bank statements or, if the administration has been conducted through, say, a professional firm's ledger account, by analysing that account. If everything has been done in cash, and no records have been kept, it may be necessary to communicate with the estate's debtors and creditors (or erstwhile ones) to find out whether they have paid or been paid. If the amounts at stake are significant and the disarray is very bad the executor may have to call in someone who is experienced in coping with incomplete records and is prepared (quickly!) to undertake the work of reconstitution.

Having finished his enquiries the executor will arrive at a stage at which the unadministered assets, the unmet commitments and the unfinished work are known. He is then in a position to make a positive contribution to the work of winding up the estate, but it is a good idea to make a record in a convenient form of the assets, commitments and outstanding work so that, in the absence of a proper estate programme, he can use that record as a platform or starting point for future operations. And such a record will obviate the need for him or anyone else to go right back to the beginning again in order to find out what has been done and still needs to be done. A suitable form, which has been found to work satisfactorily, is given in Appendix D. It may have to be varied in detail to suit particular cases, but it gives the general idea of what is necessary if time and trouble are to be saved.

If, in the course of his enquiries, the new executor finds that something has gone wrong in the course of the earlier administration (for instance, that money has been paid to the wrong person) and that the fault, if unrectified, will militate against the interests of the relatives, then unless the matter is minimal he should report to them without delay and, if possible, add his suggestions for rectification. If he chooses to leave the matter unmentioned and in abeyance until he comes to close the estate he will have allowed the distinction between his own administration and the earlier maladministration to become blurred, and inevitably some of the blame for what has happened will rub off on him — perhaps rightly so, in that the relatives should have been told. A further point, if the new executor is a professional one, is that relatives are usually less unhappy about paying out for remedial work if they know beforehand that it will be necessary than if they only learn of it when faced with the bill.

Chapter 17

DIFFICULT RELATIONSHIPS

It is evident that delay can occur at any stage (or at all stages) in the course of dealing with an estate. For reasons already explained, however, delay is more prevalent at some stages than at others. And, as the executor is the person mainly responsible for bringing the work through to a satisfactory conclusion, most of the suggestions in this book are aimed at the executor. But sometimes it is the executor who is trying to make progress and is faced with delaying tactics — perhaps not intended as such — on the part of the relatives.

Delay attributable to relatives usually occurs at two stages — near the beginning and near the end of the administration. That is not to say, of course, that they cannot maintain a campaign of harassment throughout, but the delaying effects are likely to be less during the middle stages of administration. Why should relatives delay and harass executors thus? There seem to be three reasons. One is that the relatives hope that, by creating sufficient aggro, they can gain some personal advantage at the expense of others. Another is that the relatives do not like, or do not trust, the executor and are determined to make his job as difficult as possible. Finally, their actions may be aimed at the system rather than the executor personally. Their thinking is that it is 'undemocratic' for one person to be in charge and using his discretion as compared with everything being done by relatives in committee.

In the early stages of administration the trouble tends to take the form of denying the executor access to the assets of the estate or to information about them. Refusal to hand over, say, a savings bank book may be accompanied by some such observation as "He (meaning the deceased) meant me to have this." Sometimes there is an element of truth in this assertion, in that there may have been a valid nomination or a *donatio mortis causa* (which is a lifetime gift in contemplation of, and conditional on, death), in which case the relative should be prepared to come forward with the evidence. But in the absence of any such evidence the executor must assume that the deceased's assets are to be administered as part of the estate, and must get them under control. It is quite wrong for a relative to assume that by holding on to assets wrongfully he can gain a monetary advantage. If the executor does not himself know what to do in such a case his legal advisers assuredly will, and delay will be minimised by seeking their assistance at an early stage of the dispute.

If there is trouble at a late stage of administration it is likely to be manifested in a refusal to approve the estate accounts or give the executor a proper receipt (or other form of release) for the entitlement. Obviously a genuine complaint that the accounts are wrong ought to be investigated, but fatuous objections made out of pure cussedness may have to be dealt with, subject to legal advice, by earmarking the objector's interest in the estate, perhaps in a deposit account, and distributing the rest of the funds.

The refusal to give the executor a proper receipt sometimes arises from the practice of sending out forms of receipt to be signed and returned before the money is remitted. While there may be very cogent administrative reasons for the adoption of this practice it is nevertheless open to strong objection so far as the recipients are concerned and may be regarded as provocative. If a receipt is considered necessary and the executor and the relative cannot conveniently meet to exchange remittance for receipt, then perhaps the relative can be invited to send the receipt to a trusted intermediary who will effect the exchange for him.

While it is understandable, and by no means abnormal, for the relatives to ask the executor for information about the estate, and to press if that information is not readily forthcoming, it is unlikely that the cause of expedition will be furthered by a campaign of non-co-operation with the executor, especially if it is supported by disruptive action of a quasi-industrial type. The law gives authority to the executor and likewise the law gives remedies to the relatives if that authority is used improperly. But if there is no reason to believe that anything is wrong, a policy of co-operation with the executor is more likely to bring early rewards than a campaign of militant opposition.

Chapter 18

WHAT OF THE FUTURE?

Although the basics of executorship have remained unchanged over the years — briefly, to get in the deceased's assets, meet the liabilities and distribute the balance — the machinery by which the functions are carried out has undergone considerable changes and there can be little doubt that this process will continue. Only a few decades ago legacy and succession duty disappeared from the scene, to the great relief of executors who had burned midnight oil in trying to cope with appallingly complicated residuary accounts. Estate duty, however, survived legacy and succession duty by some years; at one time the forms of affidavit and account were daunting if not actually incomprehensible, and the Revenue's reaction could be interesting, to say the least, if one inadvertently used the wrong form. However, simplification came in course of time, and even the so-called 'marginal relief' (which consisted, quite simply, of confiscating part of the estate if it created an anomaly in applying the estate duty tables) went its way. In place of estate duty came the fiendishly complicated Capital Transfer Tax which mercifully has been simplified since it was introduced in 1975. Now called Inheritance Tax, it has exemptions (notably for small estates and surviving spouses) which ensure that the majority of estates do not become enmeshed in its toils. And nowadays it is possible in some cases to obtain grants without filling in any Revenue forms at all — something quite unknown in other days. Thinking of grants, the administration bond, under which two bondsmen or an insurance company supported the application for a grant, has virtually gone; the executor no longer has to swear to the place of death; and even the amount of the estate does not have to be given exactly if it is small. All these changes are moves in the right direction, so far as the avoidance of delay is concerned.

But the changes of greatest significance are those relating to the equipment available to the executor himself. Pride of place must be given to the electronic calculator, which enables multiplication and division to be done in an instant and reduces to child's play many calculations which at one time would have taken hours to complete. Other aids have come too, such as dictation machines, plain paper copiers and word processors. Is there any scope for further change?

There surely is. Perhaps not much for executors who are already efficient, but in many quarters the mental approach to the job of administering an estate has not kept pace with today's technology. When a business acquires a computer, one of the benefits — not always recognised as such by those who feel the impact — is in forcing a review of the pen-and-ink systems in use in the office. Some of these, perhaps a trifle haphazard, have to be brought up to the standard of logic which computerised operations require. In other cases systems have to be devised where none existed before. And when the systems are right the computer has to be told what to do. It cannot just muddle through. It needs a program.

But many an executor still does muddle through. He does not use systems; he does not programme his work; everything he does is done *ad hoc*. Delays occur which anticipation could avoid. Misunderstandings arise which could be prevented by better communications within the guidelines of a proper system. So the aim for the future must be to tighten up the mental approach to the job. But even when the time taken to administer an estate has been brought down to the absolute irreducible minimum, it is quite likely that the question will still be asked:

"Why are we waiting?"

Appendix A

INFORMATION CHECKLIST

1. The deceased:

Full name
Last address
Date of death (certificate available?)
Date of birth (or age at death)
Occupation (or other description)
Domicil (i.e. country of permanent home)
Is there a will? Codicils (how many)?
Survived by spouse? child(ren)? parent(s)?

2. Persons entitled to the estate:

Full names
Full addresses
Ages, if under 18
Might someone (if so, who?) claim under inheritance law?

3. Applicant(s) for grant:

Full name(s)
Full address(es)
Occupation(s) (or other description(s))
Telephone number(s)
Have any (if so, which?) executors died?
Are any (if so, which?) executors unable/unwilling to act?

4. Deceased's assets

Bank accounts (all kinds)
Building/co-operative/friendly or other society accounts
National Savings (all kinds)
Life policies
Death grant
Unpaid salary/pension/benefit (DHSS or other)
Unexpired season ticket (refund obtainable?)
Unpresented cheques
Other forms of cash

House: address
    Freehold? If not, expiry date
    Sole owner/joint (with whom?)
    Estimated value   (or who will value?)
    Insured for £ . . . with
    Mortgaged to:- name, address, reference/account
               no., amount owing
    If no mortgage, where are deeds?

Household and personal effects:
    Estimated value
    Insured for £ . . . with
    Anything on hire/hire-purchase (from whom)?
    Car? Caravan? Boat?
    Professional valuation necessary?

Quoted investments (who will value?)
Unquoted investments (who will value?)
Business assets
Land and buildings (who will value?)
Tenancies
Accrued or apportioned income
Debts due *to* deceased (tax refund?)
Other assets (any abroad?)

5. Liabilities:

Undertaker (who?)
Other funeral expenses
Household debts
Credit card accounts
Overdraft
DHSS (re supplementary benefits)
Tax (did deceased have adviser?)
Business debts
Contingent debts (e.g. guarantees)
Other claims (advertise?)

6. Inheritance Tax queries:

Did the deceased: make any relevant lifetime gifts?
                ever have an interest in any trust
                property?
                nominate assets (e.g. National
                Savings) to anyone?
                own anything jointly?
If any answer is 'yes' or there is uncertainty the questions in the appropriate Capital Taxes Office form should be studied.

Appendix B

ESTATE ADMINISTRATION CHECKLIST

1. Pre-grant:

Urgent:
- Trace will if any; read re burial/cremation/transplant and arrange
- Consider immediate cash needs (family/business) and arrange
- Deposit season ticket (wasting asset).

Notify persons entitled to the estate (not necessary to assemble them and read the will as is done in fiction)
Obtain death certificate(s)
Locate (if possible obtain) documents and valuables
Contact landlord re surrender of tenancy
Surrender credit cards, passport, driving licence

Re specific assets:

Boat, caravan: Check insurance; Have valued?
British Savings Bonds: Confirm holding and ask for form
Building, co-op, friendly society: Ask for balance and form
Business: Arrange interim management; check insurances; obtain accounts; arrange valuations?
Car: Check (and transfer?) insurance; notify DVLC Swansea; have valued?
Cash: Note amount of loose cash — who has it? write to bank(s) for balances, etc.
Death Grant and State Pension: Apply for
Donatio Mortis Causa: obtain particulars
Effects: Check insurance; have valued?
Gifts (lifetime): Get details for Inheritance Tax if necessary; see App. A.
Life Policies: Ask for amount payable and claim form
Mortgages *to* deceased: Verify amount owing

National Giro: ask for balance and form
Pension Schemes: Ascertain benefits (dutiable?)
Premium Savings Bonds: Confirm holding and ask for form
Property abroad: Get details (appoint local correspondent?)
Property (i.e. land and buildings): Check insurances; study deeds if available; estimate value (if little at stake or sale pending); arrange valuation (other cases); ask for account (if managed by agent)
Save-as-you-earn: Send for balance and form
Savings Bank: Send for balance and form
Savings Certificates: Value (or send for value and form)
Stocks and shares: Compile list; write to companies (if unquoted); value, or have valued (if quoted)
Tax claim: Get claim form and copy of deceased's last return; prepare and submit claim
Trust: Ascertain deceased's entitlement and amount due to estate (accrued/apportioned income); get details of trusts/estates of which deceased was last trustee/executor.

Re liabilities:

Debts (including mortgage) and funeral expenses: Get details
Guarantees and contingent liabilities: Obtain and read contracts; take all possible steps to protect the estate
Hire and hire-purchase: Obtain and read contracts; ask about liability at date of death.
Income Tax Return: as for claim (see assets)

Prepare documents to apply for grant
Prepare forms for collecting/transferring assets
Arrange loan (if needed) for probate fees and Inheritance Tax
In foreign domicil cases (and some others) send account to Inland Revenue for pre-grant assessment
Lodge documents at probate registry and order office copies
Send mandates to bank

While awaiting grant:

Prepare registration letters (see post-grant, below)
Consider possible tax problems; initiate action
Are any relatives missing? initiate action
Consider which assets will be sold and which retained.

2. Post-grant:

Register original grant with Inspector of Taxes
Register copies with banks and others
Advertise for claims (if not yet done): London Gazette; local paper
Estimate cost of winding-up estate (allow for c.g.t. on sales)
Realise assets; pay debts, expenses, tax, legacies
Prepare any necessary Inheritance Tax accounts (including corrective)
Lodge accounts; adjust Inheritance Tax
Apply for Inheritance Tax clearance
Prepare assents and other documents
Obtain details of professional fees and other expenses
Ascertain final bank charges and amount available for drawing
Prepare estate account
Distribute; obtain receipts/discharges; complete assents etc.

NOTE — In programming an estate below the Duty Threshold in which the preparation of the papers to lead to the grant is expedited, some of the normal pre-grant steps (e.g. obtaining exact values at death) may be postponed and should appear in the post-grant programme.

Appendix C

ESTATE

DECISION TREE FOR SETTLING THE FUTURE OF THE BUSINESS

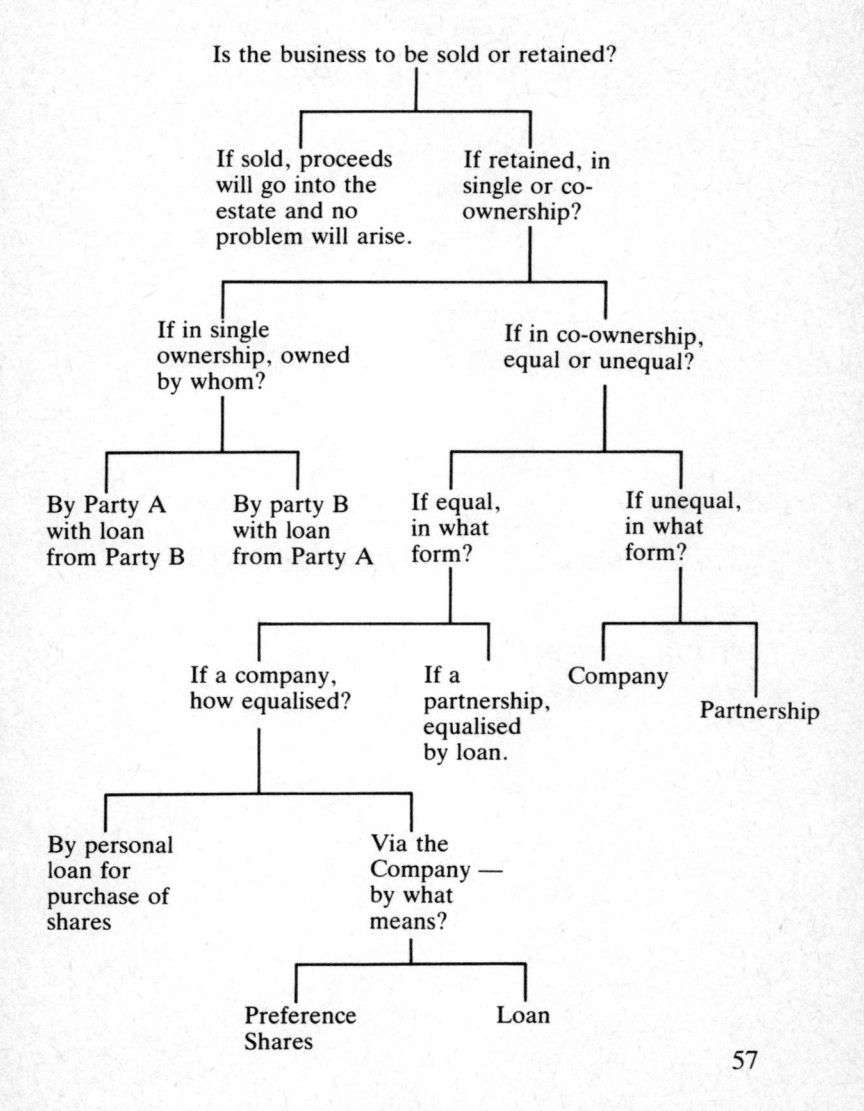

Is the business to be sold or retained?

- If sold, proceeds will go into the estate and no problem will arise.
- If retained, in single or co-ownership?
  - If in single ownership, owned by whom?
    - By Party A with loan from Party B
    - By party B with loan from Party A
  - If in co-ownership, equal or unequal?
    - If equal, in what form?
      - If a company, how equalised?
        - By personal loan for purchase of shares
        - Via the Company — by what means?
          - Preference Shares
          - Loan
      - If a partnership, equalised by loan.
    - If unequal, in what form?
      - Company
      - Partnership

Appendix D

ESTATE CONTROL

DECEASED: Mr/Mrs/Miss/Ms ─────────────

DIED ON   19 · Date of this control   19

EXORS/ADMINS/TRUSTEES (living now):

UNADMINISTERED ASSETS:

UNMET COMMITMENTS:

INHERITANCE TAX CORRECTIONS REQUIRED:

OTHER ACTION:

INDEX

Accounts
  bank 11, 12, 13, 16, 17
  estate 32–3, 46, 49, 56
  Inland Revenue 15, 17, 20, 46
Accountant 8, 43
Address
  former 28
  of Inland Revenue 24
Administration
  expenses 30, 32
  income during 24–5, 32
  without a grant 17
Advertising for
  claims 15, 26
  missing relatives 29
Annuities 21
Anticipation 15–16, 38
Approximations 13, 18
Armed forces 28
Assents 39, 56
Assessments 21, 23
Assets 10–11, 12, 13, 15, 16, 17, 18, 20, 23, 24, 30–1, 32, 52–3, 54–5
Associations, membership of 28

Bank 16, 17
  accounts 11, 12, 13, 16, 17
  charges 56
  loans, for Inheritance Tax 20
Bankers 30
Board of Inland Revenue 24
Boat 16, 53, 54
Bond 50, 54
Building Society 11, 12, 14, 54

Capital (of estate) 32
  gains tax 24
  transfer tax (CTT) 50
Car 53, 54
Caravan 16, 53, 54
Cash 11, 17

Certificates (for shares) 12, 18, 35
Charities 22
Chattels 11, 12
Checklists 10, 19, 52–3, 54–6
Claims advertising for 15, 26
Clinic 28
Club, membership of 28–9
Control, estate 58
Concealment 40
Copies of grant, official 18
Correspondence 10–13, 29, 34–5, 41–2, 45
Courts of law 40

Deceased's papers 10–11, 24, 34
Decision tree 43–4, 57
Decisions 43–4
Deeds 12, 35, 39, 55
Delay caused by relatives 48
Dependant's annuity 21
Diary 13, 19
Disarray 15, 34–5, 40, 45, 46
Discretionary trust 25
Distribution (partial) 26–7
Domicil 21, 52, 55
Donatio mortis causa 48, 54
Duties (old)
  Estate Duty 22, 50
  Legacy Duty 50
  Succession Duty 50
Duty Threshold 9, 11, 12, 13, 14, 20, 24

Electronics 24, 50–1
Employer 12, 24, 28
Equipment for filing 34–5
Estate capital 32
Estate checklist 11, 16, 54–6
Estate control 58
Estate Duty 22, 50
'Executor' 9, 36, 45

Executors, professional 7–8, 15, 33, 36–8
Exemptions (Inheritance Tax) 21–2

Filing equipment 34–5
Forces
    armed 28
    visiting 21
Former address 28
Funeral expenses 10, 11, 12, 30, 32

Gazette, London 26
Gifts, lifetime 9, 11, 21, 53, 54
Government annuity 21
Grant 9, 15, 17–19, 20, 50, 52
    administration without 17
    official copies of 15, 18, 30, 55
Guarantees 10, 53, 55

Hospital 28
House (deceased's) 11, 12, 13, 14, 53

Income during administration 24–5, 32
Income tax 11, 24, 32, 55
Information
    checklist 10, 19, 52–3
    for executor 10–14
    for relatives 13, 27, 40–1, 47
Inheritance Tax 9, 14, 15, 17, 20–2, 23, 31, 32, 50
    assessments 21, 23
    bank loans for 20
    exemptions 21–2
    instalments 21, 31
    threshold *see* Duty Threshold
Inland Revenue 13, 15, 20
    account 15, 17, 20, 46
    address 24
Inspector of Taxes 18, 24, 56
Instalments Inheritance Tax 21, 31
Insurance (missing relatives) 29
Intestacy 32, 39

Law courts 40
Legacies 21–2, 30, 56
Legacy Duty 50
Liabilities 10–11, 12, 23, 53, 55
Life policies 11, 12, 13, 54

Lifetime gifts 9, 11, 21, 53, 54
Loan for Inheritance Tax 20
London Gazette 26, 56

Marginal relief 50
Missing relatives 15, 28–9
    advertising for 29
    insurance for 29
Monitoring replies 13, 19
Mortgage 11, 12, 53, 54, 55

National purposes, gift for 22
National Savings 11, 12, 13, 17, 21, 55
Newspaper, local, advertising for claims 26, 56
Nominations 17, 48, 53

Papers (deceased's) 10–11
Partial distribution 26–7
Parties (political) 22
Pensions 21
Personal effects *see* Chattels
Picking up threads 38, 45–7
Policies (life) 11, 12, 13, 54
Political parties 22
Probate registry 9, 17, 55
'Probates' 8–9
Professional executors' fees 30
Programme 16, 56
Property outside U.K. 21, 55
Public benefit, gifts for 22

Receipts 49, 56
Rectification 47
Registration of grant 16, 18–19
'Relatives' 9, 17
    causing delay 48
    information for 13, 27, 40–1, 47
    missing 15, 28–9
Reminder form 10
Reversionary interest 21

Salary 11, 13
Sales of assets 18, 30–1
Savings, National 11, 12, 13, 17, 21, 55
Share certificates 12, 18, 35
Shareholdings 11, 12, 13, 55
Shares, unquoted 20, 55
Solicitors 8, 17, 30, 43

Spouse (surviving) 21–2, 50
Statement of trust income 25
Stockbrokers 12, 30
Succession Duty 50
Surveyors 43

Tax adviser 23–4, 53
Tax, Inheritance: *see*
  Inheritance Tax
  Capital Gains 24
  Income 11, 24, 32, 55
Taxes, Inspector of 23, 24
Telephone directory 24, 28
Threshold, Duty 9, 11, 12, 13, 14, 20
Tolerances, use of 14, 44
Trade union, membership of 28

Transfers in kind 30
Tree, decision 43–4, 57
Trust, discretionary 25
Trust funds (aggregation) 9, 11, 21
  income statement 25
Trustee Act, advertising for claims 26

Undertaker 12, 14, 31
Unquoted shares 20

Valuations 12, 53
Visiting forces 21

Will 17, 18, 32, 39, 54